FROM A:
TO
BUSINESS

TRANSITIONING ATHLETIC SKILLS TO BUSINESS SUCCESS

DARIUS ALLEN

Testimonials

"I thought the book was very good. I think it would benefit any athlete to read it. It offers cautionary tales for those with talent who will be looking at a big payday. And it will help those who are less talented by learning how to transfer the skills they learned in sports to business and the real world."

Marin Coffee – Author

" From Athletics to Business" was very inspirational to me. With me being a former NFL player it gave me the tools and guidelines to become a very successful businessman. It lays out step-by-step instructions for any athlete to transfer the same work ethic, motivation and drive they once had in their sport of choice into the work field of life. I recommend every athlete across the world to read this book it will open your eyes up to a whole new LIFE of Business......"

Joe Walker – NFL Veteran

"This book inspires, challenges, and instructs in the life after football and beyond."

Demarcus Curry – NFL Veteran

FROM ATHLETICS TO BUSINESS

"A business relationship matters as much as the results. Darius's approach to leadership and communication underscore the importance of both because it helps business leaders do the right thing in staying on task and focused. This book is a window into Darius's world of proven and practical insights, methods and tools that have made him a successful and effective business owner. I encourage every professional whether athlete or office manger to read this book. If you are looking to move to the next level this book is a must."

Phillip Owens – NFL Veteran

" This book is a must read for the transitioning athlete. After retiring for the NFL, I struggled for years trying to find my niche in corporate America. "From Athletics to Business", provides an in depth look at the correlation between athletics and business."

Perry Phenix – NFL Veteran

FROM ATHLETICS TO BUSINESS

From Athletics to Business

Transitioning Athletic Skills to Business Success

By: Darius Allen

FROM ATHLETICS TO BUSINESS

Copyright Page

Title: From Athletics to Business
Subtitle: Transitioning Athletic Skills to Business
Success
Author: Darius Allen
Published by: Darius Allen Publishing CO,
www.dariusallen.com, info@dariusallen.com, for
information address Hyperion, P.O. Box 29331
Dallas, Texas 75229

ISBN: 978-0-615-53521-0

FROM ATHLETICS TO BUSINESS

Disclaimer

This book is designed to provide information on business and motivation only. This information is provided and sold with the knowledge that the publisher and author do not offer any legal or other professional advice. In the case of a need for any such expertise, consult with the appropriate professional. This book does not contain all information available on the subject. This book has not been created to be specific to any individuals or organizations' situation or needs. Every effort has been made to make this book as accurate as possible. However, there may be typographical and or content errors. Therefore, this book should serve only as a general guide and not as the ultimate source of subject information. This book contains information that might be dated and is intended only to educate and entertain. The author and publisher shall have no liability or responsibility to any person or entity regarding any loss or damage incurred, or alleged to have incurred, directly or indirectly, by the information contained in this book. You hereby agree to be bound by this disclaimer or you may return this book within the guarantee time period for a full refund.

FROM ATHLETICS TO BUSINESS

About the Author

Darius Allen was born in Detroit, Michigan, the 3rd to last of 6 siblings and the child of General Motors plant workers. He began his football career at the age of 7, and over the years grew to love football, basketball, and track. Darius relocated with his mother and 5 of his siblings to the Dallas Fort Worth Metroplex in 1993. It was in Texas where his passion for sports grew and he developed personal relationships with athletes and coaches. When his family relocated to Atlanta, Georgia, he decided to stay behind with a high school friend's family in Texas. He eventually relocated with his family to Atlanta, and finished out his high school football career. He then went on to play college football. Darius did not receive a full scholarship; he worked odd jobs to pay for tuition and eventually started a landscaping company. Frustrated with the rat race of competing for a position, which in turn was your ticket to fame and fortune, he realized professional football was not the only way to become wealthy and he decided to forgo his senior year of football to focus on academics. Darius did not go on to play professionally, but he did use the tools he learned in sports to foster a successful career as a millionaire

FROM ATHLETICS TO BUSINESS

entrepreneur. He has been a part of many successful startup businesses ranging from Real Estate to Restaurants. Through Darius's experience, he realized how smooth the transition from athletics to business could be when you focus on the tools and knowledge you attained as an athlete and how tragic that transition can be if you do not recognize and utilize those tools. This inspired Darius to write a book, which can be used as a teaching mechanism for athletes making this transition presently or in the future, and share his knowledge through motivational speaking. In addition to being a successful entrepreneur, Darius also coaches and develops athletes' post-athletic careers.

The Dedication Page

I would like to dedicate this book to my loving Wife for her unconditional love and support. To the Faculty and Guidance Counselors within Auburn University Athletic Department. Wade Whites for going over and above your call of duty as a Junior High school coach and teaching me accountability, responsibly, and more importantly, showing me that I can change my situation. The Stout Family for taking me in as one of your own and for being a second family, excellent role models, and support system. And last but not least, to those who were not fortunate enough to make it out of the struggle of Inkster MI.

FROM ATHLETICS TO BUSINESS

Table of Contents

FROM ATHLETICS TO BUSINESS

1. The Ride

I was just like many boys my age the world over who were dreaming about becoming a professional athlete. Millions of kids grow up to be fans of athletes and see them as role models and mentors in the pursuit of happiness. However, like many other adults, I never got the opportunity to play a down in a NFL game, hit a foul ball in the major leagues, or shoot a game wining free throw on an NBA court.

The 12 Universal Attributes

The field of sports offers an individual a unique way to relieve stress and the opportunity to create lifetime relationships. This aside, the most important element of sports is to have fun. For those who venture to become career athletes, there are invaluable life skills that are developed through sport participation that can be utilized both on and off the field. These are:

- Accountability
- Attitude
- Character
- Commitment
- Competitive Perseverance
- Confidence Focus
- Leadership
- Passion

FROM ATHLETICS TO BUSINESS

- Perseverance
- Pride
- Professionalism
- Team Work

These attributes are universal amongst athletes regardless of the sport. However, athletes rarely use these skills outside the realm of sports.

Amazingly over eighty-five percent of us have participated in various types of sports and achieved some level of proficiency with these skills, whether it was in little league or as a professional athlete. However, for some reason most of us have not been able to transfer these critical skills into our professional lives.

At different points in life, we all have to step away from the competitive aspect of the game. When and how you stepped away from the game is not important. What's important are the experiences you are able to take away from the game. When an individual is able to export these skills into a business environment they will yield superior results.

Most people presume that most athletes are successful outside of sports competition. Yet the fact is most college athletes are less successful in a professional work environment than a college graduate who did not compete in athletics. I was lucky enough to observe this first hand as a student athlete at one of the most elite schools in the NCAA's South Eastern Conference. During my four years

22

at this university, they were able to produce over 20 professional athletes. Although I was not one of them, we shared the same emotional roller coaster.

The Roller Coaster

I remember the first time I was exposed to this roller coaster. I was seven years old and this was the biggest thing I had ever seen. "The Sports Rollercoaster." From a distance and at my tender age, this coaster wasn't scary in the slightest. Not only did the venture not look scary, but looked extremely fun, much like an actual carnival ride. I didn't let the endless line waiting to board deter me from dreams of riding this monster. If you made it to the end of the line you would receive the riches of the world, fame, and fortune.

As I surveyed my surroundings in line, I notice that everyone in line didn't actually ride the rollercoaster.

The beginning of the line was a joyful time. Most every kid there was ecstatic to even participate in the line. Everyone was allowed to enter the line, but as I inched closer to the top I noticed disheartened kids inauspiciously stepping out of line. A select few became tired and uninterested and chose to leave the line. Most were forced to step out of the line because of physical requirements. It was as if every few steps leading to the rollercoaster revealed new physical requirements to remain in line such as height, weight, speed, and strength. The list of qualifications went on and on.

Some kids had natural born talent while others worked extra hard and struggled to keep up. If you were lucky enough to meet the physical requirements, you weren't completely out of the woods just yet. Without any warning and during any time in line, an injury would claim a kid and extract him or her from line. Some would return to the line where they were, some would be forced to begin farther back in the line, and others were not able to physically recover from the injury and were not seen in line again.

By the time the kids reach the end of the line they had become adolescents. At this stage, not only are these young men and women measured by their athletic performance, they are assessed on their academic performance as well. At this point you are no longer on the stairway leading to the rollercoaster; you're on top of the platform where the next step is boarding the ride.

In many sports this platform would be recognized as college. Every year you see individuals who look just like you getting on and off the coaster. As a kid at the very beginning of the line, you were not aware of all the obstacles that were involved in boarding this ride. You just looked up at the tall pinnacles in amazement and told yourself you will be on that ride one day. Like millions of others, that "one day" never came for me. My dreams of riding the rollercoaster died near the very end of the line on the platform.

Since I worked so hard to get to the platform, I stayed there for a while. I stayed there for several reasons. One reason was hope; I hoped for the chance to ride. A second reason was to watch. I watched the friends and others that had been in line with me get their opportunity to embark on that monster.

Watching my friends and teammates board the coaster was exciting. Some lasted longer than others. During my observations, I discovered the selection process also involved luck and politics. Who would have known? When I first entered that line as a kid, I knew nothing about this aspect of the game. I just figured if you were physically better than others you're competing against you would automatically get to ride. However I have seen guys whose talent and dedication was head and shoulders above other players denied the chance. I also saw mediocre players welcomed aboard.

If you didn't make the ride you exited alongside those getting off the ride. Yet at this point I did not yet realize that those who did not make the ride and those who did were exiting in the same place: the real world. While the ride had presented the lucky few with the riches of the world, fame, and fortune, many of these athletes ended up in far worse situations and conditions than those of us who never rode at all.

FROM ATHLETICS TO BUSINESS

As I left the ride and the amusement park of sports competition altogether, I found that many of us who had competed in line all those years had also not been able to adapt or use the skills we had obtained to compete in the 'real world.'

2. Why Do They Fail?

"Pity the man who inherits a million and isn't a millionaire. Here's what would be pitiful, if your income grew and you didn't." - Jim Rohn

The majority of athletes that make 'the ride' are well paid. Those that perform consistently earn some of the highest incomes in the world. Salaries have risen progressively over the last few decades. In addition they can earn bonuses and boatloads of money from product endorsements. Yet history shows most professional athletes are broke only six years after retiring from sports. The facts are staggering. According to *Sports Illustrated*, after only two years of retirement, 78% of former NFL players have filed bankruptcy or are suffering under financial duress regardless of how much money they made.

NBA and Major League Baseball players are no different. The ways these athletes blow their money are strikingly comparable.

MLB players Johnny Damon of the Yankees, Jacoby Ellsbury of the Red Sox, Mike Pelfrey of the Mets, and Scott Eyre of the Phillies found that some of their money is part of the $8 billion fraud allegedly perpetrated by Texas financier Robert Allen Stanford.

Pelfrey reported to the *New York Post* that 99% of his fortune is frozen; Eyre said he is broke, and the team advanced him a portion of his $2 million salary.

Why do so many athletes fail financially and even more fail to achieve success outside of sports?

PERCEPTION

There is a perception that comes with newfound wealth. Once someone who comes from poor or modest means believes they are wealthy or a millionaire, they often see this newfound position as a state of being. After all, being poor is often a state of being that can seem almost impossible to change. While wealth is at the other end of the spectrum the perception that this state is permanent can be just as strong.

When compared to well-paid professional athletes, big lottery winners do not fair much better. Estimates are that half of all of these winners end up in bankruptcy at some point after collecting the money. According to Chelmsford wealth counselor Szifra Birke, roughly one-third of lottery winners find themselves in serious financial trouble or bankrupt within five years of winning.

While some of these lottery winners fall prey to misplaced trust when placing control of their winnings in the hands of financial advisors or others, and some of these winners lose everything because of family matters, many overspend because they do not understand the law of relativity.

THE LAW OF RELATIVITY

As of this writing the US Government is over fourteen trillion dollars in debt and climbing. That is a number most of us cannot fathom:

14,000,000,000,000.

And that's in English.

A trillion in many other countries has eighteen zeroes:

14,000,000,000,000,000,000.

In addition the US operates on a trade deficit, meaning we spend more than we make.

In 2010, the US census bureau reported that each credit card holder has an average credit card debt of $5,100 and that is projected to reach $6,500 by 2011 (source: www.money-zine.com/Financial-Planning/Debt-Consolidation/Consumer-Debt-Statistics).

The average credit card charge over 16% annual interest and requires a minimum monthly payment that will not retire the principal for decades on the average household balance. Even an elementary financial student will tell you this is a poor financial choice.

FROM ATHLETICS TO BUSINESS

Credit card companies have long preyed on Americans and the human desire for instant gratification. This desire does not change when income increases or the credit card limit is raised. In fact, consumer behavior shows the desire only grows.

The same principle is true for lottery winners and athletes. The more they can suddenly seemingly afford, the more they acquire.

The Law of Relativity is a simple principle to conceive, yet seemingly nearly impossible for most people to practice. No matter how much income you are making or how much money you have, if you spend more than those amounts you will run out of money.

Factor in taxes; cost of living and the perception of athletic immortality and that there will be income for years and bigger paydays down the road. No professional athlete believes he or she will be playing just a few years or that they could be the victims of a career ending injury.

We cannot expect lottery winners or high paid professional athletes will manage their money any better than the general public or the US Government without specific financial education and adapting a financial mantra of spending less than they have or are making.

LACK OF KNOWLEDGE

Many athletes are not versed in financial management. Participating in line for 'the ride' often requires all their mental and physical fortitude and they have no reason to learn financial responsibility. They have not had the money to make investments, and are too young to have thought about retirement much less become educated about planning.

Upon signing a contract, they often become instant millionaires and are in need of immediate advice.

"With athletes, there's an extraordinary metamorphosis of financial challenge," says agent Leigh Steinberg, who has represented the NFL's No. 1 pick a record eight times. "Coming off college scholarships, they probably haven't even learned the basics of budgeting or keeping receipts."

"Athletes have a different set of challenges from, say, entertainers," states Michael Seymour, money manager and the founder of Philadelphia-based UNI Private Wealth Strategies. "There's a far shorter peak earnings period [in sports] than in any other profession, and in many cases they lack the time and desire to understand and monitor their investments."

Johnny Unitas was a millionaire in the 1960s, yet a chain of mismanaged bowling alleys and a printed-circuit-board company led him to bankruptcy by 1991. Fortunately, he survived by working for appearance fees from collector exhibitions.

Bjorn Borg won six French Opens and five Wimbledon titles and retired a millionaire at age 27. A few years later he was so broke he was forced to sell his trophies just to survive when his fashion label business failed. Borg attempted to return to the tour to earn a living but was embarrassed on the court.

Wizards forward Andray Blatche claims to be so bad with money, that despite an NBA contract, he was forced to sleep some nights at the Verizon Center because he couldn't pay his rent.

Dwayne Wade's estimated earnings between 2003 and 2010 are well over $50 million. Wade partnered with two others to open a sports restaurant in 2008. Wade's investors pushed to expand across the southeast before Wade thought the business was ready. Due to the disagreement he allegedly didn't make promised promotional appearances. His two established restaurants closed for business in 2009 with a $25 million lawsuit against him.

The only athlete in history to win the Heisman Trophy twice as the nation's best collegiate football player, Archie Griffin had a short and lackluster career as professional athlete.

Though he was a millionaire, his chain of athletic shoe stores collapsed and he entered personal bankruptcy about the time he participated in Super Bowl XVI. After his career on the field ended, he did return to his alma mater and earned an MBA.

Despite earning $42 million from 1996 through 2009 in the NFL, Mushin Muhammad's entertainment business was sued in 2008 for defaulting on credit card payments. He was forced to put his home up for sale for only 70% of the asking price to cover legal expenses.

Track champion Marion Jones states she was broke in 2007, even though she earned seven figures from endorsements after the 2000 Sydney Olympics. She lost her $2.5 million North Carolina home in 2006, and her total liquid assets at the time were valued at less than $2,000.

The lack of financial knowledge also leads to hiring the wrong advisers, and trusting them too much.

MISPLACED TRUST

Trust can be misplaced due to a lack of knowledge as mentioned, a lack of attention, or for emotional reasons.

A newly signed athlete has many obligations and requests. Focusing on an athletic career itself can be all consuming. Then there are the family obligations, friends, approaches from strangers, sports memorabilia contracts, fans, endorsement considerations, lawyers, and the press. Anyone stepping up to the plate claiming to have your financial interests at heart or an investment recommendation from a family member or friend can be seen as a welcome hand to lighten the load of one less responsibility. This lack of attention to investigation and verification can be devastating later.

Estimates are that Joe Louis earned $4.6M from 1935 to 1952 in the ring. He later started the Joe Louis Restaurant, Joe Louis Milk Company, Joe Louis Punch, and Louis-Rower P.R. Firm. He banked on his name to secure his financial future, yet a corrupt business manager and several bad business investments left this champ with chump change.

Emotional Reasons

When a long-time friend or family member claims to have an inside investment tip or the savvy to handle finances, saying no can sometimes be difficult.

Con artists have regularly preyed on the fortunes of athletes. The NFL Players Association states that from 1999 to 2002 at least 78 players lost more than $42 million total to financial advisers with questionable backgrounds:

Luigi DiFonzo was a former felon who claimed he was an Italian count and defrauded athletes such as Hall of Fame running back Eric Dickerson.

34

William (Tank) Black was an NFL agent who built a pyramid scheme that robbed about $15 million from more than a dozen players, including Patriots running back Fred Taylor

Kirk Wright was a hedge fund manager who was convicted on 47 counts of fraud and money laundering for more than $150 million and the list of victims included eight NFL players.

LIFE AND FAMILY MATTERS

Many of us have an idea or fantasy about what life would be like if we were very rich. We perceive all our problems would be gone. The fact is while checks can solve certain problems, there are many life issues that cannot be solved with money or can be made worse. Relationships with friends, family, associates and acquaintances can be made more complicated by money. Large amounts of money can cause people to become distrustful of loved ones and lifelong friends and weary of the motives of new acquaintances.

When professional athletes, lottery winners, and others with newfound wealth come into money, family matters do not cease to exist. In fact they are often exacerbated. A divorce will usually involve more property, more money, more people and more decisions. The issues of life and family matters can also become public, costing these people far more than unknown individuals.

FROM ATHLETICS TO BUSINESS

Raghib Ramadian Ismail is a retired NFL player nicknamed "The Rocket" for his speed. In 1996, when Panthers owner Jerry Richardson—a former NFL flanker turned businessman—addressed his players, one of them asked, 'What's the most dangerous thing that could happen to us financially?' "Without blinking an eye," Ismail recalls, "Mr. Richardson said, 'Divorce.'"

By the way, Rocket Ismail lost a fortune by funding a movie; the music label COZ Records; a cosmetics procedure; a startup that would create nationwide phone-card dispensers; a Rock N' Roll Café; a restaurant in New England; and three shops called 'It's in the Name,' where visitors could buy framed calligraphies of names or proverbs they chose.

SOCIETY AND PEER PRESSURE

Society and peers often measure success by consumption. The bigger the mansion, the more expensive the cars, clothes, and jewelry, the greater the success. And none of these items comes with a tag or sign that tells onlookers whether the item is owned or purchased on credit. So athletes and their spouses or girl and boyfriends can look even more successful than their bank balances or incomes might reflect.

In addition, organizations, friends, family members, and strangers will expect and ask for help in the form of financial assistance, time, and endorsement or other use of the athlete's name. The pressure to give in to these requests can be overwhelming. Often there is guilt associated with money and many athletes must learn when to say no.

Mike Tyson had earned more than $300 million and went broke and filed for bankruptcy in 2003. Tyson spent his fortune on depreciating luxury cars, lavish jewelry and Bengal tigers.

When former baseball star Jack Clark filed for bankruptcy in 1992, he was under contract for $8.7 million contract with the Red Sox. Clark's bankruptcy records show at the time that he had $6.7 million in debt, which included payments in default on 17 cars.

TANGIBLE APPEAL

Just as expensive cars, clothes, jewelry and homes are appealing and interpreted as wealth, so are tangible investments. Nightclubs, car dealerships, or high-end restaurants are far more alluring and easy to impress with than even the best stock portfolio.

Athletes are often tempted by the tangible attraction of an investment more than the logical black and white numbers of ROI (Return On Investment.)

Bill Buckner earned an estimated $6M from 1977 to 1989 as a major league baseball player. He then opened Bill

Buckner Dodge Chrysler Jeep. He filed for personal bankruptcy just two years after opening.

Deuce McAllister earned an estimated $36 million from 2001 to 2008 in the NFL. McAllister's Mississippi car dealership sought bankruptcy protection in 2009 and was sued by Nissan. McAllister countersued, claiming Nissan should have known he had no business acumen, as he was an athlete.

BEHAVIORAL MISTAKES

An athlete depends on his or her body for performance on the field or court and often for a reputation for off the field earnings. Behavioral infractions against the sport or that result in breaking the law can have grave financial consequences.

Drugs

Josh Hamilton
Baseball star Josh Hamilton put a $4 million signing bonus up his nose in the form of powder cocaine, as reported in *Maxim.*

Chris Andersen
Chris "Birdman" Andersen partied away his $289,000 2001 NBA signing bonus and four years later got expelled

for two years for unspecified drug use, according to *ESPN*, and lost a $3.5 million annual salary.

Ricky Williams
NFL star Ricky Williams paid an estimated $8.6 million for breach of contract for failing drug tests and then received a one-year suspension.

Criminal Behavior
Michael Vick spent 18 months in prison for supporting dog fighting and killing dogs. The star NFL quarterbacks also went broke. He lost millions of dollars in salary and endorsements, and spent his fortune on legal fees, fines and supporting family and friends. Recently a judge approved a plan for him to repay creditors $20 million.

Behavioral mistakes have many consequences and costs for athletes. NFL first-round pick Adam 'Pac man' Jones was suspended by the NFL for off-field incidents. He missed the entire season in 2007 and was later released by the Dallas Cowboys. Jones lost a four-year contract with the Cowboys worth $13.3 million.

Endorsements can often be the most lucrative income for many athletes and can be lost instantly due to behavioral mistakes. Olympic champion Michael Phelps' picture was taken as he smoked marijuana from a bong, costing him his Kellogg's endorsement deal and financial support from USA Swimming.

FROM ATHLETICS TO BUSINESS

I'll stop here because I am sure you get the point, however, this list of examples unfortunately goes on and on.

Irresponsible Relationships and Parenting

Athletes are often sought as sexual partners for bragging rights, parenting a child, or other unethical motives. This can present tempting scenarios, especially for young men. Parenting multiple children with different women can have costly consequences.

Travis Henry

The *New York Times* has reported that former NFL player Travis Henry, a running back who played for three teams from 2001 to 2007, has fathered nine children and each one by a different mother. Some of the children are practically the same age. Henry claims he is broke, and cannot pay the estimated $170,000. In annual child support he now owes.

Evander Holyfield

Boxing champion Evander Holyfield is another example. Holyfield has grossed more than $248 million in the ring. In addition to failed investments, he has also experienced two divorces and has come close to losing his home because of child support payments close to $500,000 a year.

FROM ATHLETICS TO BUSINESS

Vance Johnson
Many kids envy the position once held by former NFL player Vance Johnson. He admits to beating his first wife unconscious, ramming his car into his second wife's vehicle and fathering seven children by various women.

Johnson played for the Denver Broncos from 1985 to 1993 and was part of the trio of receivers known as the Three Amigos.

His abusive treatment of women was well known and he has paid hundreds of thousands of dollars in paternity and alimony payments.

Despite making millions of dollars in his football career Johnson's 2,636-square-foot home on a little over an acre of land in Colorado went into foreclosure in 2008 and he was taken to court by Land Rover Capital Group for failing to make payments on a vehicle.

Johnson has had financial problems related to criminal behavior besides battering women. He was wanted in Rifle, Colorado for missing a court date related to a 2001 incident when he had allegedly written two bad checks. This was a crime Johnson also committed while playing in college at the University of Arizona.

Vin Baker
Vin Baker's estimated earnings between 1993 and 2006 are a whopping $93 million. His Fish House restaurants

collapsed, leaving him and his parents in debt. Gambling and alcoholism reportedly contributed to his $93 million loss.

DENIAL

An athlete's performance is usually public and a record, and reputation can be affected by just one event. When an athlete experiences failure he or she often ignores a weakness and concentrates on success. The more successful they become in sports, often the more infallible they feel. Their egos become intertwined and dependent on performance and athletic and social status. Facing or admitting defeat in another area of their lives can become unbearable, so they deny the problem.

This often happens when an athlete begins to experience financial difficulty. The longer they deny the issue and fail to seek help, the further their situation can veer off course, thus leading to bankruptcy that might have been avoided.

Lenny Dykstra

The headline read "Lenny Dykstra refuses to admit that he can't fund his magazine and brokerage company despite earning $35M on the field."

FROM ATHLETICS TO BUSINESS

Lenny Dykstra, known as "Nails" for his hardcore attitude on the field, earned more than $34 million from 1985 to1998. He paid almost $20 million to buy Wayne Gretzky's house, and purchased a high-end private jet. He pledged millions to fund his glossy magazine and brokerage firm. He ended up in a tangled mess of legal trouble and was forced to seek Chapter 11 protection.

Athlete's fail for a number of reasons, most of which are preventable. Most of the time, they are their own worst enemies. The good news here is that by taking accountability, athletes have the power to control their finances and financial future.

3. The Athlete's Marketable Skills and Attributes

"The measure of who we are is what we do with what we have." - Vince Lombardi

Regardless of what you think of Vince Lombardi, the Green Bay Packers, or even professional football, the man was a master of motivation and his talents to win football games is rivaled only by his witty way with words. His often poignant and sometimes controversial statements made him one of the most quoted coaches of all time. His quips were often delivered off the cuff and sometimes amid outbursts of seeming rage, but always with fervent passion.

The wisdom in Lombardi's words, as peppered throughout this chapter, were often as philosophical and applicable for life as they were for the motivation of his team at half time in the locker room, responding to a curt reporter, one-on-one behind closed doors with a player, or standing over an exhausted athlete collapsed on the field of play.

"Football is like life - it requires perseverance, self-denial, hard work, sacrifice, dedication and respect for authority." - Vince Lombardi

FROM ATHLETICS TO BUSINESS

The Real World Skills

While there is no shortage of athletes who have failed financially and personally off the field or after retiring from sports, professional athletes have no shortage of marketable and real world skills for other forms of employment and business. In fact amateur, college and professional athletes, and anyone who has spent time playing organized sports, has an abundance of marketable skills.

Athletes possess similar desirable attributes. Some of these characteristics and behaviors exist in people before they become athletes. These are further developed by sports and other attributes and instilled by the sports environment, requirements, and coaches and team members.

The degree of each attribute varies from one individual to the next. Some are stronger in certain attributes than others.

All of these attributes are encouraged in most business environments and can serve the athlete well in the business world.

Many athletes have not taken inventory of these skills, are unaware they have them, or lack the information and capacity to transfer their knowledge, skills, and abilities from sports to life.

FROM ATHLETICS TO BUSINESS

"The quality of a person's life is in direct proportion to their commitment to excellence, regardless of their chosen field of endeavor."
- Vince Lombardi

Team Work

"People who work together will win, whether it be against complex football defenses, or the problems of modern society." - Vince Lombardi

Teamwork is one of the first skills that come to mind for most people when assessing athletes. Most sports involve teamwork. Sure there are individual games, such as tennis, boxing, golf, figure skating, gymnastics, and so on although even these activities often involve teams. If you were to participate in any one of those sports in school, at the Olympics, or under most other circumstances, you would be on a team.

"Individual commitment to a group effort - that is what makes a team work, a company work, a society work, a civilization work." - Vince Lombardi

The team skills athletes learn are highly valuable in the world of business. Individuals are the components of the team engine that drives the group to success. In order to achieve the highest performance, there are four primary elements required for this success that are instilled in the individual athlete. These are:

• Dedication and Commitment

- Motivation and Determination
- Orientation toward results
- Autonomy

There is no shortage of team success stories in sports.

The Miracle on Ice

"It may just be the single most indelible moment in all of U.S. sports history," said *Sports Illustrated* about Team USA's unforeseen gold medal in hockey at the 1980 Winter Olympics.

On February 22, 1980, a young group of Americans took down the mighty Red Machine from the USSR. The year before, the Soviet team had trampled the NHL All Stars 6-0. The Soviets completely dominated the 1979 World Championship.

Herb Brooks was the coach, himself a veteran of two Olympic teams. The Americans were underdogs, but the team was scrappy and competitive. But in a pre-Olympic exhibition game against the Soviets, the Americans were easily defeated 10-3.

Brooks spent a year-and-a-half cultivating the team. He held grueling tryout camps, which included psychological tests. After finally making his selections, the team spent four months playing a pounding schedule of exhibition games across Europe and North America.

FROM ATHLETICS TO BUSINESS

The team could not match the Europeans' skill. So Brooks concentrated on speed, conditioning and discipline. Brooks challenged each player physically and verbally, often in shouting matches.

At Lake Placid, Team USA fought against Sweden for a tie. Then gained momentum with wins over Norway, Romania, and Germany. The Soviets had gone undefeated.

The US hoped to avoid playing the Soviets as long as possible for medal contention, but drew them first. If you have never seen the series of games, you are missing out. Every game was dramatic.

In game one as the Soviets mounted a final charge, Broadcaster Al Michaels made the most famous call in all American sports: "Eleven seconds. You got ten seconds, the countdown going on right now. Five seconds left in the game! Do you believe in miracles? Yes!"

With millions of Americans watching, the team sealed the gold. The "Miracle On Ice" became America's greatest sports achievement of the 20th century. A few years later Hollywood made the movie *Miracle.*

Leadership

"Leaders are made, they are not born. They are made by hard effort, which is the price which all of us must pay to achieve any goal that is worthwhile." - Vince Lombardi

Leadership skills are highly valuable in the business world for business owners, entrepreneurs and employees. Leadership involves many skills and an intricate harmony of combining those skills. Athletes learn to be leaders from leaders or coaches. They learn to be flexible to quickly accept new tactics and new roles. Many athletes are cross-trained to change roles or positions on a team in a moment's notice. This flexibility builds appreciation for the roles of other team members and enables the athletes to see how the duties of different positions affect other team members. Cross training also makes a team less vulnerable from the loss or absence of a team member.

Athletes learn the value of peer behavior. Often a strong team develops with the aid of peer pressure. Performance of athletes is often directed at satisfying supervisors, some coaches encourage peer motivation and discipline. Team members are dependent on one another for success. From this dependency spawns trust and expectations.

The natural abilities of athletes are continually developed. Team success includes developing the strengths or skills that are unique to each team member. This is critical in the realm of business.

Athletes face various challenges that test both physical and mental fortitude.

Athletes must plan and implement under extreme deadlines. Years of training and months of planning can come down to one second in sports. Working with a sense of urgency is a requirement for survival and success in business. Speed of implementation is a must in business and action is dependent on timing, and hesitation can be costly.

Whether they are aware or not, athletes have an abundance of leadership skills and attributes that will be critical and beneficial in business, though not all of the aspects of these skills will transfer to every business application. Business owners, managers and executives are limited by budgets, different rules or laws, and report to many entities such as accounting departments, tax authorities, government agencies, customers, and a board of directors.

Athletes are taught to recognize their capabilities, problem-solving skills, and how to assess their talents and benefit a team. This assessment experience will enable the athlete to quickly determine what they need to learn and what areas of expertise to outsource in business.

Leaders Recognize Leadership Qualities

The "Miracle of Richfield," happened during the 1975-76 NBA season when Bill Fitch coached the overachieving Cavaliers to their first winning season and playoffs. In fact during his NBA career, Fitch saw every challenge as an opportunity to become better, no matter how hopeless things seemed. In his career in the NBA he turned every team he coached into a playoff contender.

Years before while working as a scout for the Atlanta Braves, he stopped in the bleachers in Williston, N.D., and saw a lanky, young man playing basketball. He noted how this player set picks, executed good defense and made use of his unusually long arms. The player had limited offensive skill yet had a flair for the ball. This short observation from those bleachers stuck in his mind. Later when Fitch became coach of the University of North Dakota's basketball team, he recruited that player. That player was Phil Jackson, who was a second round draft pick for the New York Knicks in 1967. Jackson was a reliable player but spent time plagued with injuries.

Fitch had seen something else in Jackson that day in the bleachers in Williston. He recognized a leader, who sacrificed stats for setting effective picks, and a cerebral player.

For coaching career spanning 22 years, Jackson achieved more than anyone could have ever expected. Nobody expected a low-level professional league tactician would turn out to be one of the greatest coaches in NBA history, except Fitch. At the end of his career, after coaching eleven championships, Jackson thanked Fitch for believing in him.

Fitch claims his greatest achievements are not his winning record or championships. They are the players he had the opportunity to influence. Fitch states he witnessed two miracles in his life: The "Miracle of Richfield", and a day in the bleachers of Williston, N.D.

Successful Leadership Skills in Sports Transfer Into Business

Head coach Joe Gibbs of the Washington Redskins gave his team the second best team record in NFL history. Over twelve years he led them to four Super Bowls and three world championships.

Joe went on to start an auto racing empire and become a popular speaker. Joe tells his life story openly and shares his trials and triumphs in football and auto racing, and how sports made him a success in the most important game of all, the game of life.

4. Skills and Attributes A-H

Ability to Listen, Follow Instructions, and Heed Advice

Athletes quickly learn to listen to coaches and follow instructions. They see experienced peers and coaches as mentors and take their advice on the sport. These abilities rank at the top for employees and leaders in business.

Ability to Comprehend, Interpret and Adhere to Rules

Any sports participant either learns and follows the rules or gets thrown out of the game. Athletes learn how to excel within the parameters of their sport. Business is no different. There are tax rules, accounting practices, laws, marketing methods, and so on that will allow profits when adhered to and inflict penalties when broken.

Ability to Measure Effectiveness

"Don't rate potential over performance." - Jim Fassel

"A particular shot or way of moving the ball can be a player's personal signature, but efficiency of performance is what wins the game for the team." - Pat Riley

Knowing how to be the most effective is vital in sports and a career after athletics. The professional athlete knows well that activity does equate to productivity. Because athletes are results oriented, they know how to measure effectiveness of benefits and work to optimize practice and performance.

Accountability
"What to do with a mistake: recognize it, admit it, learn from it, forget It." - Dean Smith

Athletes hold themselves accountable and will admit and take responsibility for mistakes. They learn to do this without eroding their confidence.

Developing a sense of personal accountability is absolutely essential to business success. When a person holds himself or herself accountable, those around him or her are encouraged to do the same. In order to help develop accountability, expectations must be in place.

Sports teams often have well-defined expectations for the team and individual team members. Setting expectations and then achieving them produces results that give customers, employees, and investors' great confidence in the leader.

Until a person can take responsibility for their own actions and the consequences   they will often struggle throughout life and frequently claim victim status. Victim status promotes helplessness, whereas accountability empowers a person. Entrepreneurship, business ownership, and leadership all require personal accountability.

Aligned Goals and Ideology

"The most important part of motivating players is telling them the truth, telling them what it's going to take for them to have to win, telling them to play for the name on the front of their shirt, not the one on the back of their shirt." -Tommy Lasorda

Athletes learn how to align their goals with those of a team and how to help others do the same?

Attention to Details

To achieve optimum performance, athletes must pay great attention to details. For instance, in order to make one move, swinging a golf club, a golfer often analyzes:

- grip
- Wrist turning
- Stance
- Hip position
- Knee flex
- Head position
- Eye focus
- Swing follow through
- Club head
- Club face

FROM ATHLETICS TO BUSINESS

- Club strike
- Club position
- Back swing
- Down swing
- Strike angle
- Environment factors
- Mental focus
- Emotional control
- Physical strength and ability

And a host of other possibilities. The devil is in the details. In addition, athletes must also learn strategies, the strength and weaknesses of teammates and opponents, statistics, play environments, the physics on equipment such as a bat or baseball, the effects of weather conditions on equipment and play surfaces and many more details.

Neglecting to consider details important can cause catastrophic failure. One second, one inch, and a single point can be the difference between winning and losing a Championship in sports.

Details are as important as the sum of the parts. Business survives and succeeds upon attention to details.

Athletes are trained to pay great attention to details. Any other pursuit after sports will be benefited by this attribute.

Nurture this habit during your athletic career and realize the difference between attention to details and obsession with details. When you see the big picture and understand that every image is made up of many small details, you can keep each point in perspective.

Autonomy

Athletes learn to develop the ability to endeavor to understand, rather than requiring that others make themselves understood. They learn to work toward the finish line using their talents and skills within defined boundaries without direct supervision. This is critical for business management, ownership or the entrepreneur. Most entrepreneurs and business owners do not have a cheering section when they report to work each day. Being self-sufficient and a self-starter is a must.

Collaboration

Athletes look to coaches, advisors, physical therapists, doctors and others to find ways to connect and funnel energy for a purpose.

Realize the strong parallel of communicating with your personal team of coaches, advisors, physical therapists, doctors and others and how you orchestrate and funnel knowledge and energy for your purpose. Observe your leaders and how they develop optimal collaboration between teammates, and the professionals who support the team.

The ability to collaborate with the knowledge and abilities of others is critical for business success.

Communication

A greater part of communication is listening. Athletes learn to listen to coaches, teammates, and other professionals. Business requires the   communication of ideas, directions, and goals in a way people will understand in order to get them to act as desired.

Listening is as important as speaking in communicating. Great leaders know how to listen. Develop your listening ability with coaches, teammates, and other professionals.

Learn how to express ideas and concepts in a way that inspires and motivates the people with whom you interact.

Confidence

 "Confidence is contagious. So is lack of confidence." - Vince Lombardi

Champions seldom lack self-esteem in their sport. Confidence pushed them on, allows them to hear opposing views, gives them the ability to persuade others, and to win.

True self-confidence is based on a developed self-perspective that recognizes strengths and shortcomings.

Winning athletes have a confidence that is fueled by an awareness of shortcomings and limitations and how to deal with them, rather than denial. They believe in their strengths and the power to overcome their opponents.

Most any champion athlete has self-confidence. Often an athlete facing the loss of sports and a change into an unknown career will experience an unfamiliar lull in self-confidence. They can be leaving a career where they have been on top and starting a new one at the bottom.

During your sports career, take stock of the times you might have been unsure of yourself or when your confidence waivered. Record what restored your assurance and you can draw on these times after you leave sports.

Confidence in Action

Pat Riley led the L.A. Lakers to four consecutive NBA Finals appearances. In 1987, Riley coached a Lakers team considered one of the best teams of all-time that included Hall of Famers Magic Johnson, James Worthy and Kareem Abdul-Jabbar, Michael Cooper, Byron Scott, A. C. Green, Mychal Thompson, and Kurt Rambis.

One of Riley's most famous moments was when he guaranteed fans a repeat championship during the Lakers' championship parade in downtown Los Angeles. Though that next year, 1988, the season did not produce as many wins, but the Lakers did win the NBA title, becoming the first team in 19 years to repeat as champions, making good on Riley's promise.

In 1969, the American Football League team the New York Jets were given little chance of winning Super Bowl III. They were facing the NFL's Baltimore Colts. The point spread was very high against them. Sports writers predicted a blowout.

Quarterback Joe Namath rallied his team and AFL supporters at a Super Bowl dinner by announcing, "The Jets will win on Sunday, and I guarantee you." Namath completed 17 of 28 passes for 206 yards and the aroused Jets made big defensive plays to stun the Colts 16-7, completing a super season.

Comprehension of Winning and Losing

"You can't measure success if you have never failed." -Steffi Graf

Sports teach the value of winning and losing or success and failure. Because of the knowledge found in losing, athletes learn to cope and rebound. Athletes strive to win but can appreciate winning because of losing and the journey.

Conflict Management

Athletes experience how conflict is addressed and differences resolved. These instances can serve as opportunities to learn how to solve issues in business. Conflict is a part of doing business. There is internal conflict amongst employees and team members and external conflict between a business and suppliers and vendors, customers, contractors, and governing bodies.

Courage

"Without cancer, I never would have won a single Tour de France. Cancer taught me a plan for more purposeful living, and that in turn taught me how to train and to win more purposefully. It taught me that pain has a reason and that sometimes the experience of losing things - whether health or a car or an old sense of self - has its own value in the scheme of life. Pain and loss are great enhancers." - Lance Armstrong

Courage is required to have faith in visions and goals despite circumstances and when others cast doubt. Courage is an attribute needed to lead throughout life.

The obstacles and challenges athletes have faced have come in many shapes and forms.

Courage in Action

While Shay Oberg was an athlete throughout her childhood; she was never on a level playing field. While others were on the team and battling for positions, Oberg repeatedly demonstrated courage just for the chance to play on a team. She had to fight to even be considered for athletics and a chance to show she could play sports.

FROM ATHLETICS TO BUSINESS

Later Oberg became the right fielder for Southwestern Oregon Community College and at 5-foot-9 inches can outhustle, out-throw and outfield almost anyone she's played against at the junior college level. Oberg steals bases in less than three seconds, often bunts her way on base and is known for her quick throws to the plate. She is an exceptional player and... she does all of this with one hand.

Jackie Robinson, often most famous for his play on the baseball field, swallowed his tremendous pride and absorbed untold mental and verbal abuse in 1945 to break the racial barrier that had existed with separate leagues for blacks and whites for sixty years.

In the 1940s, Branch Rickey, the general manager of the Brooklyn Dodgers, sought out Robinson for possible inclusion in Brooklyn's International League farm club, the Montreal Royals.

Rickey wanted to be sure Robinson could withstand the inevitable racial abuse that would come. During an interview on August 28, 1945, Rickey asked Robinson if he could face the racial onslaught without taking the bait and getting angry. Robinson had previous run-ins with law enforcement and in the military. Robinson was shocked at Rickey's inquiry and asked, "Are you looking for a Negro who is afraid to fight back?"
Rickey responded that he needed a Negro player with the courage and guts enough not to fight back.

Robinson agreed and went on to play more than ten seasons, and in six World Series, with the Dodgers. He was picked for six consecutive All-Star Games, was 1947 MLB Rookie of the Year and the National League Most Valuable Player in 1949. Robinson was inducted into the Baseball Hall of Fame in 1962 and in 1997; Major League Baseball retired his number, 42, from the entire league.

Creativity
Athletes often improve their performance through creativity. They must think of solutions to overcome challenges, obstacles, and opponents. They think of new ways to motivate themselves.

Business requires creative thinking on a daily basis. Expand your creative thinking by searching for and developing your own new solutions for obstacles and challenges as they arise.

Curiosity and a Desire to Learn
Athletes have a burning desire to learn all they can about their game and performance. They welcome the knowledge of others and learn from coaches and peers. This eager longing to learn and seek information is critical to business. Business leaders stay informed of current events and the activities of other leaders, adversaries and allies. Be aware of this natural curiosity and work to maintain this throughout life.

Decision Making
Decision-making might be the most vital skill in business. Fortunes are made and lost based on single decisions. Businesses require owners to make dozens and even hundreds of decisions a day. No detail is too small when a choice is presented and livelihood is on the line. Even the smallest decision can have an impactful effect.

Contrary to what many fans might think, athletes make many decisions. In addition to college, career, and contractual decisions, there are second by second decisions being made during performances. Athletes learn to weigh the consequences of decisions and inactivity.

Delegating
As part of a team, athletes witness delegation of duties often based on the capabilities, strengths, and weaknesses of individuals. This enables them to effectively assign responsibilities and authority in business.

Dependable and Reliable
Great business leaders do what they say and follow through. Athletes can be counted on to show up week after week and get the job done.

Desire to Help Others
Many athletes have the desire to help others. This attribute influences many new athletes and is a great characteristic in business. Many individual athletes have

started nonprofit organizations, as have groups of athletes and entire teams.

The San Francisco 49ers Academy in East Palo Alto has received continued contributions and commitments from the entire 49ers organization. The San Francisco 49ers Academy is a school for 6th, 7th and 8th grade students.

Carlos Emmons of the NY Giants and Takeo Spikes of the Buffalo Bills established 51 Ways for Charity, Inc. They support families of children that have been diagnosed with cancer and/or blood disorders.

The Anthony Weaver Foundation was founded in 2004 and provides financial and personal aid to children in the Greater Baltimore Area and Saratoga Springs, NY. Anthony's college nickname was the "Dream Weaver" which is appropriate now as he is making the dreams of children come true.

The Brett Favre Forward Foundation provides aid to disadvantaged children in Wisconsin and Mississippi. Three annual fundraising events are held to raise funds: The Brett Favre Celebrity Golf Tournament; The Brett Favre Celebrity Softball Tournament; and The Brett Favre Steak Dinner. The Foundation works hand in hand with other nonprofits such as Special Olympics, Make A Wish Foundation, and the Boys and Girls Club.

Derek Jeter's Turn 2 Foundation works to keep young people away from drugs and alcohol and "TURN 2" better choices.

The Andre Agassi Charitable Foundation presents recreational and educational opportunities for at-risk boys and girls.

The Jackie Robinson Foundation was founded in 1973 by Rachel Robinson and awards four-year college scholarships to academically gifted students with financial need, enabling them to attend the college of their choice.

Will Shields, Kansas City Chiefs All-Pro Right Guard, along with his wife, Senia, created the "Will To Succeed" Foundation in 1993. They work to improve the lives of abused, battered and neglected women and children.

The list of charitable organizations founded by athletes would fill a book itself.

Dedication and Commitment

"Luck has nothing to do with it, because I have spent many, many hours, countless hours, on the court working for my one moment in time, not knowing when it would come." - Serena Williams

Definition of commitment is: "the

trait of sincere and steadfast fixity of purpose, the act of binding yourself (intellectually or emotionally) to a course of action."

FROM ATHLETICS TO BUSINESS

Commitment requires athletes to stick with their practice routines, stay in the game, and play with the team even during the most challenging of times.

Committing to improving, for instance, requires athletes measure their performance and set goals to better individual and often team results. Athletes commit themselves to excellence, and continue working toward being the best regardless of the obstacles that might arise.

Excellence has magnetic appeal which people are drawn to and inspired by. Athletes want to be a member of something excellent. Professional sports fans often choose their favorite teams for a variety of reasons including: geography, childhood, or heritage, to name a few. Many fans support a team or athlete because they are the best. Fans and athletes are resilient and are also often relentless in the pursuit of excellence. This dedication and commitment can take them through some of the toughest times.

A football team can win a long grueling season only to suffer heartbreak from a dismal loss in the Super Bowl. Yet time after time, every member of a losing team will show up for training camp ready to go again, and the team will often still sell every seat in the stadium the next season.

Professional sports are successful economically because of fans. Fans are so committed to teams they will buy and wear hats and shirts with their team insignias, attend or

FROM ATHLETICS TO BUSINESS

watch game after game, and are emotionally affected by each win or loss. They place ownership on their favorite team's achievements. You can often hear them shouting how they won after their team beats out a competitor. Yet their contribution was only as a spectator.

Allegiance can often be so strong that only hope of a championship keeps them tied. The Chicago Cubs, for example, have not won a World Championship in over a century. Yet Cub fans are some of the most dedicated fans in professional baseball.

Coaches harness the commitment of players through motivation and helping each team member and the team reaches excellence.

Many people have become leaders, though the great leaders have not happened by chance. Great leaders made a decision and commitment to be great leaders. They gather knowledge and study what is needed to be great leader. They implement and practice to improve leadership skills. Athletes are often exposed to many strong leadership principles.

Empathy
Athletes are also exposed to empathy. Good coaches, trainers, and other advisors work to understand the athlete's challenges and provide support and solutions.

These leaders know the difference between empathy and sympathy and how to express empathy.

Flexibility

Successful athletes are adaptable to change. They learn to accept and seek out input from others and are eager to consider changes based on the suggestions and ideas. Learning the balance of flexibility in day-to-day activity contributes to understanding the need to place attention on items in order of priority. Because new needs arrive daily in business, this will be a valuable attribute in their next career.

Goal Setting and Planning

"A man has to have goals - for a day, for a lifetime - and that was mine, to have people say, 'There goes Ted Williams, the greatest hitter who ever lived.'" - Ted Williams

Athletes have a great understanding of visions or goals. They compete in a game for the short-term goal of winning and work long and hard for the vision of a championship. They set realistic goals based on assessments of their skills and or the capabilities of their team. They create step-by-step plans and timelines for achieving goals.

Sports are crammed with stories of team and personal goal setting and achievement. Most every athlete, championship, medal and trophy has a goal-setting story.

Behind most businesses everywhere you will find a person or team of people who have visions or goals. The ability to set realistic goals based on capabilities and resources is imperative for business success. Evaluate how coaches and teams establish step-by-step plans and assign responsibility for duties. Keep notes about your personal goal-setting process and a list of your successes. Work to improve how you define goals and keep them in the forefront of your activity.

Enthusiasm and Energy

"If you aren't fired with enthusiasm, you will be fired with enthusiasm." - Vince Lombardi

Athletes work in an environment of energy and enthusiasm. Coaches work to boost each individual's level of energy and the team's adrenaline as needed.

Athletes see firsthand how energy levels are affected by others and performance. They learn to draw out enthusiasm in themselves in the tough times to raise the level of performance of themselves and those around them. This ability is a coveted strength in the world of business.

Frank Bettger was playing minor league baseball in Johnstown, Pennsylvania in the 1920s. While he believed himself to be ambitious, he was called into the office one day for the surprise of his life. He was fired for being lazy. Frank was shocked. "I'm not lazy," he told the manager.

"You sure looked lazy. You looked like a tired twenty-year veteran on the and off the field," his manager responded.

FROM ATHLETICS TO BUSINESS

"I'm nervous and afraid, and a way for me to hide my nervousness and fear is to be nonchalant, and take it easy," Frank retorted.

Later Frank was offered a job playing for a team in New Haven, Connecticut. As he packed his bags, he vowed to be the most enthusiastic player on that team. No one would ever accuse him of being lazy again.

The moment Frank arrived for practice he ran onto the field. He made a habit of being the first player on the field and the first player back to the dugout between each inning. He threw the ball around with such force that players burned their hands catching his throws.

The first game he stole third base, and slid into the third baseman so hard he knocked the ball out of his glove and ran on to score the winning run. The next day the New Haven paper printed, "The new player, Bettger, is a barrel of enthusiasm." Frank got a new nickname, "Pep Bettger." He cut the article out of the paper and sent a copy to the manager who fired him.

Frank was eventually called up to play third base for the St. Louis Cardinals. After a short time, his athletic career was cut short due to an injury.

"My enthusiasm almost entirely overcame my fear. In fact my nervousness began to work for me, and I played far better than I ever thought I was capable of playing. (If you are nervous be thankful. Don't hold it back. Turn it on. Let your nerves work for you.) My enthusiasm affected the

FROM ATHLETICS TO BUSINESS

other players on the team, and they too became enthusiastic." – Frank Bettger

Frank took his lesson about enthusiasm and the same energy to his career life after sports and became a top world-renowned insurance salesman. You can read his inspiring story in his book: *How I Raised Myself From Failure to Success In Selling.*

5. Skills and Attributes I-Z

Information Management
Athletes are often unaware of how they can identify, locate, assimilate, organize, and analyze relevant information. They watch training films, movies of games, and read information about nutrition, athleticism, inspirational stories, and personal, team, and competitor statistics. They become students of their game. They locate, identify, assimilate and organize the information that can help them and analyze how to implement the knowledge.

This same process of utilizing information can be duplicated in any career.

Innovative
Athletes are prepared to think in fresh ways and seek answers in unfamiliar territory. They learn to adapt new information to their routines in order to make improvements.

Insightful
Athletes learn the valuable attribute of insight by reflecting on events and understanding the positions of others.

Integrity

"Integrity is telling myself the truth. And honesty is telling the truth to other people." - Spencer Johnson

Sports help athletes build values. There are established principles of right and wrong.

Keen Sense of Justice

A keen sense of justice and fairness is instilled through sports. Athletes must know the rules of their games and how to respect and appeal decisions. This sense transfers well into the business world and will earn the respect of associates, employees, and clients. This will create a business climate that encourages the expression of ideas and promotes innovation.

Knowledge of Leadership Styles

Because athletes are often exposed to several or more coaches, they become aware of different leadership styles. This should instill an appreciation of leadership and encourage them to seek out leadership knowledge.

Leadership

At the very least, the leadership skills an athlete witnesses during a professional career can benefit most any career after sports. Leadership skills are valued in most employment positions and often priceless in entrepreneurial roles.

During your sports career, observe the commitment to lead made by coaches and managers and understand the abilities required and sacrifices made.

Modesty

"A lot of times I find that people who are blessed with the most talent don't ever develop that attitude, and the ones who aren't blessed in that way are the most competitive and have the biggest heart." - Tom Brady

The greatest athletes often win and accomplish feats while thinking in terms beyond mere personal gain. Athletes learn to become accountable for their mistakes, learn to make corrections, and do not seek out accolades for their accomplishments. Many athletes learn to see themselves as leaders beyond their egos.

Motivation, Initiative, and Determination

"The difference between a successful person and others is not a lack of strength, not a lack of knowledge, but rather a lack of will."
- Vince Lombardi

Many people think athletes receive all or most of their motivation from coaches. Others believe high paid professional athletes show up for the money. Coaches can be very inspiring and money exciting, yet the fact is most any athlete will tell you that motivation must come from within. There is no coach there when an athlete wakes in the morning, sore, stiff, and tired and must still get to the gym and workout or drive to a tough practice. And every high paid athlete was at one time not paid a single dollar for his or her work.

Successful athletes are self-motivated from within. They desire to achieve excellence and consistently challenge themselves, pushing past yesterday's limits. Their determination is driven by a passionate and enthusiastic desire to be the best.

Athletes learn to take the initiative at every opportunity by being proactive. They become accustom to being ready and willing to accept responsibility and this empowers them. They are motivated about every goal and exude energy. They work in and understand how to create an environment in which people can flourish. They know how to inspire excitement that motivates others.

Orientation Toward Results

"Some of us will do our jobs well and some will not, but we will be judged by only one thing—the result." - Vince Lombardi

Athletes become skilled at being results-oriented. They focus not just on completing the task at hand, but ensuring that the final result fulfills the purpose of the activity.

Optimism

"Everything negative - pressure, challenges - is all an opportunity for me to rise." - Kobe Bryant

Optimism is an attitude. Champions have winning attitudes of optimism. Problems that arise are seen as challenges of opportunity. They have optimism so ingrained within them that they will muster all their strength and continue to fight with a belief in overcoming, no matter how the odds might seem stacked against them.

Organized

Athletes are trained in organization through regimented practice, competition schedules, records and statistics, and equipment. They know to compete effectively they must be organized. Athletes utilize technology, other people, and any applicable tools to get and stay organized. They recognize that organization is a practiced activity and not a state.

Passion

"Guys ask me, don't I get burned out? How can you get burned out doing something you love?"
- Tommy Lasorda

Athletes are full of passion for the pursuit of their sport. They approach their plans, problems, and challenges with vigor so strong often others are persuaded to follow them. Athletes believe in themselves and their visions. They get excited discussing them.

Patience

"A man who is a master of patience is master of everything else." - George Savile

"There are three secrets to managing. The first secret is to have patience. The second is to be patient. And the third and most important secret is patience." - Chuck Tanner

Athletes acquire patience. They must wait for their turn and often depend on many others for their performance. They learn to be patient as they implement plans and work towards goals.

Persistence

"Winners never quit and quitters never win."
- Vince Lombardi

Athletes will not go far without a strong ability to persist. They persist to compete to the very end of every competition and then go home to practice for the next event. They realize the value of persistence and overcome obstacle after obstacle to obtain their achievements. Athletes reach deep inside themselves for the determination to push on when challenges arise or things don't go as planned.

Persuasive

Athletes often have developed strong persuasive skills. They work to convince others to let them participate, to win over coaches, referees, and umpires, and to lead others to follow them.

Planning

"The reason most people never reach their goals is that they don't define them, or ever seriously consider them as believable or achievable. Winners can tell you where they are going, what they plan to do along the way, and who will be sharing the adventure with them." - Denis Waitley

Athletes usually have solid planning skills. They create achievable goals and the plans to get them there. They work with others to develop personal and team tactics and strategies to achieve their goals.

Perceive and Achieve Goals

Often from the very first game they play or time they compete, sports participants discover the importance of understanding goals and how to achieve them.

Power

Athletes are often aware of their source of power. They work to understand this power and how to wield it effectively.

Problem-solving

Athletes can evaluate themselves, search for solutions for improvement or issues, and resolve problems quickly and effectively.

Risk Assessment Ability and Courage to Take Risks

"Never surrender opportunity for security." - Branch Rickey

Risks are required for rewards and athletes know this. They develop the ability to assess risks and risk tolerance of themselves and those around them.

Self-Respect

"Respect your efforts, respect yourself. Self-respect leads to self-discipline. When you have both firmly under your belt, that's real power."
- Clint Eastwood

Playing sports can lead to developing self-esteem, which incorporates self-respect. Each time a participant achieves a goal, a building block is placed in the foundation of self-respect. This self-esteem has pulled many children and young people away from the effects of detrimental environments.

Self-Discipline

"We all have dreams. But in order to make dreams come into reality, it takes an awful lot of determination, dedication, self-discipline, and effort." - Jesse Owens

Self-discipline allows people to embrace accountability. Athletes oblige themselves to uphold the expectations set for them. They do this for themselves, coaches, fans, and fellow teammates.

Discipline in this sense is a corrective action and not about consequences for actions. Discipline requires identifying actions that do not best help reach expectations.

Athletes develop self-discipline that becomes so instilled within them their actions become automatic. As Ralph Waldo Emerson once said, "Your actions speak so loudly I can't even hear you anymore."

In addition to what others might expect of them, athletes set their own standards of excellence.

Sense of Urgency

Because of the nature of competition, athletes have a sense of urgency about them. They have an agenda for their goals. A sense of urgency is often listed as one of the top traits of highly successful people.

Sensitivity and Respect

Sports teach respect and validation of the needs of others. Team members often aid each other in improvement and see the assistance to the individual as a benefit to themselves and the team.

Solidarity

Athletes recognize individuals and see teams acting as a unit of one. They inspire others with a sense of solidarity.

Stamina

"Just because your muscles start to protest, doesn't mean you have to listen." - Dianne Holum

Most athletes have to work to further develop physical, mental, and emotional stamina for the demands of their game. They understand the requirements and sacrifices to reach their goals.

Steadfast
"Success demands singleness of purpose."
- Vince Lombardi

Athletes work consistently toward their goals in an often unwavering manner. They act calmly in the face of interference or catastrophe. They are steadfastly resolved to see things through, even in the most difficult circumstances.

In business, an owner or entrepreneur must act calmly in the face of adversity or catastrophe and always be resolved to see things through.

Strong Work Ethics
"The dictionary is the only place that success comes before work. Hard work is the price we must pay for success. I think you can accomplish anything if you're willing to pay the price."
-Vince Lombardi

Athletes typically have developed strong work ethics that will serve them well in business as an owner or employee.

Time Management
Sports are based on time. There are specific time requirements for most competitions, time kept for certain pursuits and records, appointments, and time schedules for competitions, games, meetings, and practices. Athletes know the value of time management.

83

Tolerance
Athletes are tolerant of ambiguity and adversity. They can recognize that tolerance presents opportunities.

Visionary
"We would accomplish many more things if we did not think of them as impossible."
- Vince Lombardi

Athletes look to the future and create new goals and plans to reach them. They see themselves as champions and often visualize winning.

Willingness to Step Beyond the Comfort Zone
"If somebody says no to you, or if you get cut, you push harder. Michael Jordan was cut his first year, but he came back and he was the best ever. That is what you have to have. The attitude that I'm going to show everybody, I'm going to work hard to get better and better." - Magic Johnson

Athletes continually push themselves beyond yesterday's limits and outside of their comfort zones. By exercising their flexibility, they become stronger and learn the rewards of risk.

Entrepreneurs know their comfort levels with risk and know how to access risk. They often step outside of their comfort zones to take these risks and reap the rewards.

6. Why Pursue College

Earning Potential of an Athlete is Short Term

History and current statistics show most all athletes will need additional sources of income after sports. Most athletic careers are short lived and they do not earn or keep enough money to retire for life. There are numerous reasons why the athletic career window is short. The average lengths of sports careers for professional athletes are as follows:

NFL

According the NFL Players Association, the average career of an NFL player is **3.3 years**. This is because of injury, retirement, suspension, and being cut by their team. Even the best of athletes are at the end of their careers in the NFL before forty years of age.

NBA

Player turnover in the NBA is fast and furious. If you are thinking you will have a long NBA career you need to know that the average NBA player at the start of the 2010 season was 26.77 years old and had **4.84 years** of NBA experience. Over half of NBA players are rookies or have less than four years of experience.

A long NBA career is highly unlikely. **Only 46** players on opening day in 2010 had more than 10 years of NBA experience, and *only 9* had been in the NBA more than 15 years.

MLB

According to a study conducted by the University of Colorado at Boulder, the average length of a professional baseball career is **5.6 years** and one in five position players will have only a one year career in baseball.

NHL

The National Hockey League has one of the shortest average lengths for professional careers: only **2.66 years**.

Injuries End Careers

Athletes will fight hard and usually find pursuing a professional sports career extremely difficult. They will battle all the way through the ranks of high school and college to even get a chance to play. Then one play or even a practice routine can result in a severe injury. Then all they can do is work hard to rehab their injury and hope and pray they will play again. Many athletes fortunate to get back in the game after an injury finds they can never perform again as they once did.

While the odds of professional athletes attaining enough financial success during their athletic careers to sustain them for a lifetime are stacked against them due to all the reasons for failure described earlier, there is also the injury factor.

At the same time young people often believe they are invincible and athletes maybe even more so, the truth is that anyone is susceptible to a career-ending injury at any time and *athletes even more so.*

There is a long list of well-known athletes whose careers were cut short by injuries and many lesser-known athletes who were out before they really started. Careers ended early leave potential unknown and earnings lost.

In 1991 Bo Jackson was on top of the world as an All-Star major league baseball player, all world NFL running back, and reaping the benefits of becoming a pop culture icon. He then suffered a devastating hip injury in an NFL playoff game. Bo's injury became more complicated when he developed a blood flow disease and required a hip replacement. He never played football again. He did return to baseball in 1993, and won Comeback Player of the Year. However, his injury forced him to quit sports altogether after that.

FROM ATHLETICS TO BUSINESS

The great Tony Conigliaro was the youngest player to ever hit 100 home runs and be selected to the All Star Team and then he was hit in the face by a pitch. He sat out two seasons and then attempted to play again and won Come Back Player of the Year. However his injuries kept him from continuing his success.

The famous Gayle Sayers was the NFL Rookie of the Year in 1965, yet played only four seasons due to knee injuries that became apparent in a 1968 game while playing for the Chicago Bears. He made a desperate attempt at rehab, which was not successful.

While Don Mattingly was a six-time all-star and nine-time gold-glover, a 1987 back injury for all practical purposes was the demise of his career.

Joe Namath was the 1965 Rookie of the Year and the first NFL quarterback to pass for 4,000 yards in a 14-game season. Yet he underwent four knee operations and had to repeatedly have his knees drained at halftimes. From 1970 to 1973, Namath missed 30 games and finally had to quit.

Terrell Davis carried the Denver Broncos to two Super Bowl wins and then the dream ended with a blown ACL in 1998.

Mark Bavaro was Phil Simms go-to-guy and a 1996 Monday Night Football game made Bavaro a legend when he caught a pass and ran down field with five 49ers on his back. Bad knees basically knocked him out of the game and his skills were diminished after the age of 29.

Mark Prior was the second pick of the 2001 amateur draft and was touted as the best pitching prospect. He was signed to a record $10.5 million contract by the Cubs. In his first full season, he posted an 18-6 record with 245 strikeouts and was named to the All-Star team.

The next season, Prior was beleaguered with injuries. An Achilles tendon injury, fractured elbow, and shoulder injury all required reconstructive surgery. At 30 he is trying to salvage a once promising career playing on a minor league team.

There were great expectations when the Athletics drafted Mark Mulder. He racked up an impressive 72-32 record from 2001-2004 and led the A's to four straight postseason appearances. Then in 2006 while playing with the St. Louis Cardinals, he was diagnosed with a career ending torn rotator cuff.

These are just a few examples of the many career ending-injuries that have sent athletes home before their time. Athletes depend on their physical prowess and invest in strict nutrition and exercise regimens to stay in peak condition. But injuries come with the territory.

Not all injuries are sports related. Jay Williams, the 2002 number two draft pick was in a motorcycle accident after only one year of play. He suffered a severe leg injury and was waived by the Chicago Bulls and although he attempted a comeback with the Nets in 2006, his career was over.

Professional athletes are also susceptible to the many health conditions that plague the general public. Ernie Davis was the Browns 1962 draft choice, yet he never got the chance to play. Despite a brilliant career at Syracuse, he was diagnosed with leukemia.

Athletes need a back up career plan, whether as an employee or entrepreneur.

Education Benefits

The fact that people with college degrees have better career opportunities than their counterparts is broadly accepted. Yet how do you convince a young athlete that education is important when they have stars in their eyes and even worse, when they have a well-paying contract in their pocket?

Here are two convincing arguments:

1) According to the NFL Players Association, NFL players with college degrees make between 20% and 30% more than players who left school early to enter the NFL.

2) The NFLPA now reports that players with degrees will have careers that endure about 50% longer than those

without degrees. This is attributed to the fact that most young NFL players need the time in college to mature.

In addition, completion of education before the end of the athlete's career instills great confidence for the transition.

7. Strategic Planning During the Athlete Career

Having an understanding of your identity away from the game and a life purpose can help you determine where your passion lies for a second career. When you know your internal strengths, weaknesses, interests, values, and passions, you can plan your next dream. An Assessment Coach can help you get in shape for the game of life.

A business coach is valuable after sports for the same reason a coach is needed in sports. Having a trusted advisor who can steer you in the right direction and motivate you can increase your level of success.

Develop your second passion while you are in the game. While you are still in the game is the time to explore and create a plan to understand your other passions and talents. Take action now and you can take control of your life after sports.

One important factor in preparing for the next chapter of the athlete's career life after sports requires first recognizing the valuable skills, abilities, and attributes that are built and or enhanced by sports as described in chapters three and four. When you are aware of these skills and attributes, then you need to understand how they will benefit you in your next career.

Find Great Mentors and Examples

You don't need to discover how to be an entrepreneur or have a career after sports from scratch. Look at other athletes that have moved on with businesses and careers. Seek out people that exemplify the attitudes, virtues, and habits you want to develop and the success you desire. Meet with them, watch how they work, and use them as mentors.

Look for the skills, attributes, and principles in your mentors, coaches and other leaders and how they utilize them. Work to establish and develop these same talents within yourself during your athletic career.

Developing Skills for Careers and Business

LEARN

Developing leadership qualities during your athletic career can serve you well in the future, whether you become an employee or entrepreneur. Many of the most valuable skills come from a commitment to personal development.

Learn to Think in Tangible Terms

Enthusiasm, a positive attitude, and goals are abstract concepts and because of that can be difficult to maintain.

93

Relate your abstract concepts and goals and develop tangible relations.

For each characteristic you desire to build, create five concrete acts that demonstrate that attitude in action.

You can list things you would do on a usual basis, or how you would respond to specific situations.

For instance, if you desire to be more personable, list five actions you could do to develop this attribute. Now imagine yourself performing these actions. Write down what you would do and say. Then begin practicing these actions at every opportunity.

Learn to Set Smart Goals

Athletes know the power of goal setting. Set clearly defined goals for yourself. Make your goals measurable with benchmarks to measure your progress. Your goals should be realistic or attainable. Set time limits for each goal. Visualize the actions that will help you achieve your desired outcomes.

Write It All Down

Recording your goals on paper and posting them where you will see them makes them more concrete. In addition, writing things down creates a psychological feedback loop that reinforces your goals.

Learn to Make Habits

Changes often need to start small in order to become habits. Perform actions that reinforce the habits you seek to develop and practice them each day. Many experts believe you must perform an action for 21 days in a row to create a habit.

Set Aside Time for Personal Development

Set aside time each day to work on your mindset explicitly. Whenever possible retreat to a quiet place, free of distractions, and write down any results, issues, successes, questions and observations. Consistency is important.

Personal development also includes learning and increasing your knowledge of the industry you are targeting, business, and entrepreneurship principles.

8. Exit Strategies

When should professional athletes begin planning their exit (from the sports career) strategy? The day they sign their first professional sports contract.

The moment a young person begins a career in getting paid to play, they should plan for the day they will stop playing. Because of the uncertainty of a sports career due to possible injury, diminished skills, strikes, changes in team management, and the host of financial and other issues so many athletes have experienced as described earlier, having a plan in place for post-sports from the beginning is the smartest move.

As with many instant successes or millionaires, the mindset the athlete often has upon signing that first contract is that they have made it. They are there and will never have to worry about money again. Even though the success is not really instant because these athletes have typically worked a lifetime to become pros, the act of signing that first contract and the emotion is immediate.

Planning from the beginning can prevent a great deal of tragedy and loss and create a sense of security that will allow the athlete to better focus on their game instead of reacting to arising financial crises or worrying about their future.

FROM ATHLETICS TO BUSINESS

As history shows, often for professional athletes, how they fair post-sports depends not just on how much they make but also in how much they keep.

There are several things that athletes need to consider on day one.

1) Instant money does not necessitate instant purchases. While there might be some basic provisions a new athlete is in immediately of, usually no large purchases are of critical importance. So decide exactly what you really need and how much that will cost before you spend one cent. The difference between needs and wants is monumental.

A want can be described as a strong desire or inclination for.

A need is a legitimate physical or psychological requirement for health and welfare.

2) Instant wealth does not necessitate instant credit. While instant wealth commonly generates instant offers of credit lines, most new professional athletes do not need credit. Avoiding credit of any kind for at least the first year might be a wise move.

3) Instant money does not necessitate instant investments. Athletes are often tempted to instantly invest their money. Advisors and others typically tell them that

they are losing money by not investing immediately. The fact is investments come with varying degrees of risk and often the faster they invest the sooner they lose their money.

Any money beyond living expenses can be temporarily placed in a savings account or perhaps a one-year CD (certificate of deposit.) While this will probably earn a minimal amount of interest, this will also be very low to almost no risk.

While an athlete starting out in a sports career will be very busy, spending some time learning about the risks of investments during that first year can make the difference between retiring or transitioning to a new career one day comfortable or needing to start over again financially. Remember the earlier examples of athletes who have lost enormous amounts of cash. No amount of money makes you immune to complete loss.

1) Realize that every amount of money is a finite number. No matter how much you feel you have, the emotional amount might be different than reality.

2) As most athletes have much shorter careers than other professions and then is often needed to produce income, your life after sports could easily be fifty years. Imagine that your career ends at the age of thirty-five. How much income or money will you need to live the lifestyle you desire annually? Now multiply that number times fifty. That is the minimum amount of money you will need

because there are often unforeseen expenses, cost of living rises due to inflation, and your career could end well before you are thirty-five years old.

3) Plan on having only the money you possess now when you exit sports. While future income in sports might seem guaranteed, as in life, there are no guarantees.

4) Learn about the differences between assets and liabilities. The best way to leave sports with no liabilities is to never acquire any. This means no loans. Even borrowing money for real estate and investing are liabilities that often carry great risk.

5) Learn the difference between passive and active investment income. While you do not need to become a financial adviser to make great investments, you will need some general knowledge. Many athletes that have ended up penniless or bankrupt made enough money during their careers to have lived comfortably for the rest of their lives by only placing their money in the bank! Yet they invested in active investments.

Businesses are usually active investments. They are active because they will require your activity. Absentee owner businesses are often absent of one other important factor: profit. While a business or businesses can be a great post-sports career they are often not the best investment for an active athlete.

FROM ATHLETICS TO BUSINESS

Passive investments usually have varying degrees of less risk. No matter what you hear, there is nothing wrong with planning a retirement from day one with a majority of your money in low risk passive investments. No matter how tempting the stock market might seem, for every winner there is one, or many more losers.

6) Take your time learning about investing and developing a network of financial advisors and business mentors. Keep in contact with those who prove fruitful, as many of them can be quite valuable in your post-sports career.

7) Think about what you want to do after your professional sports career. If you cannot imagine being away from the game, think about careers that will keep you close to the sport or even a volunteer activity that will fit the bill.

A sports card and memorabilia shop, radio or TV sportscaster, coach, manager, physical therapist, or sports agent are all possibilities. Keep your eyes open for opportunities by watching what other retired athletes are doing.

8) Prepare yourself for when the time approaches to leave sports. You will need to adjust to the dimming of the limelight and even starting at the bottom in a new career and environment. Swallow your pride. With the right attitude you can see this as an adventure and learn a great deal from new experiences and new people.

9. The Right Choice: Employee or Entrepreneur

The decision of becoming an employee or entrepreneur is personal and unique for each individual. There are common and different skills required for an employee versus an entrepreneur.

The Mindset

Due to the nature of sports publicity, many athletes become celebrities. These celebrated athletes are held in high esteem. Leaving this realm of attention and giving up the spotlight to begin a career can be somewhat embarrassing and even humiliating for many former athletes.

For this reason some individuals will choose to be an entrepreneur for the wrong reasons. Rather than face the possible damage to their egos by becoming an employee, they choose business ownership for the esteem of being the boss.

Each athlete will need to make this very personal decision; however, basing this more on your skills rather than emotion will increase your chances of success. The failure of a business can often bring more feelings of shame than working as an employee.

101

The Entrepreneur

The mindset of the successful entrepreneur runs parallel to the professional athlete. What are the defining sets of traits, attitudes, and habits that are found in entrepreneurs?

When a business fails some entrepreneurs will point a finger of blame at issues with the economy, employees, or other influences. This attitude might have had a great deal to do with why the business did not succeed. When a business venture has failed, the best things an entrepreneur can do is ask what could be done better the next time, and learn from the mistakes. The ability to learn from mistakes is what enables entrepreneurs to ultimately achieve that success. This is the same principle utilized in most sports programs and athletes often have this skill instilled in their thinking, making entrepreneurship a seemingly natural transition from sports.

Entrepreneurs know they are responsible for their businesses just like coaches are responsible for their teams. You win some and you lose some and entrepreneurs succeed, and sometimes they do not.

Businesses require common characteristics and skills from their owners and specific businesses often require additional specific skills.

Some businesses require working many hours, some require heavy renegotiating skills, and other require regular contact with suppliers or clients.

The Entrepreneur Versus the Employee Mindset

Making the transition from athlete to business owner requires applying the traits, habits, and attitudes learned in sports and adapting them to the business environment.

An employee will have a safety net of a weekly paycheck and a well-defined set of responsibilities, whereas an entrepreneur will often have a wide scope of duties and might sometimes need to forego pay. The risk and rewards of entrepreneurship can be greater and are often the challenge a former competitive athlete needs.

The role of an employee is often about tasks. Entrepreneurship requires leadership ability. Leadership is more than the strategic fundamentals of organization, individuals, and getting things done. Leadership is about influence and innovation. Leadership is about envisioning where the business or team needs to go and guiding them in the right direction.

An employee is assigned a series of tasks that he or she must accomplish frequently by working with other people. A leader has a vision, and works to achieve that vision often by working through other people and influencing them.

An entrepreneur must motivate people to take action and provide them with the tools they need to get the job done. An entrepreneur is a leader and leadership is not about what you do as much as who you are and what you inspire others to be.

Developing the leadership skills required to be an entrepreneur takes time and energy. A professional athlete will typically have been exposed to and acquired many leadership skills.

While the terms entrepreneur and employee are not the same, good entrepreneurs tend to also be good employees because they know how to achieve results.

Leadership

Leadership is about the leader, though leadership is not about one defining personality trait that makes leaders. Leadership is developed and not something you are born with.

Leaders come in all shapes and sizes and from varied backgrounds. There are common threads among great leaders.

Characteristics of Great Entrepreneurs

Great leaders are not self-centered. Great leaders do not micromanage. Great leaders are humble and lead to serve others.

The Servant Leader

"The servant-leader is servant first. It begins with the natural feeling that one wants to serve, to serve first. Then conscious choice brings one to aspire to lead. That person is sharply different from one who is leader first, perhaps because of the need to assuage an unusual power drive or to acquire material possessions ... The leader-first and the servant-first are two extreme types. Between them there are shadings and blends that are part of the infinite variety of human nature." - Robert K. Greenleaf

Characteristics of a Servant Leader

In *The Servant Leader Within*, Larry C. Spears, CEO of the Robert K. Greenleaf Center for Servant-Leadership, outlines the ten characteristics or skills of a true servant leader:

1. A Servant Leader is a Good Listener. A servant leader listens to others to identify and clarify.

2. Servant Leaders are Empathetic.
They work to see things from the point of view of others. This understanding enables them to correct problematic behaviors without persecution and without rejecting the follower.

3. A Servant Leader is a Healer.

4. Servant Leaders are Aware.

5. The Servant Leader is Persuasive. Servant leaders use influence, and not authority, to lead.

6. Servant Leaders are able to Conceptualize. Servant leaders look beyond the day-to-day realities of life and see the big picture.

7. Servant Leaders Possess Great Foresight. A servant leader has a knack for predicting likely outcomes by weighing lessons learned with present realities and the potential consequences of each decision.

8. The Servant Leader is a Steward. A servant leader's primary commitment is to serve the needs of others in order to help them reach their full potential and the organization's goals.

9. Servant Leaders are Committed to the Growth of their People. A servant leader strives to nurture the personal, professional, and spiritual growth of the team. Spears states "servant leaders believe that people have an

intrinsic value beyond their tangible contributions as workers."

10. The Servant Leader Works to Build Community. The servant leaders work to develop a sense of community among the employees of an organization.

A servant leader serves his followers before he attempts to lead. A servant leader strives to extend and improve himself in order to lead his followers as best he can. Great leaders work to raise their game, improve their character, and become better people so that they can better serve those around them.

In sports, coaches do much more than just watching games and taking notes. They are mentally in every game making decisions, offering support, adjusting plays and positions, addressing issues. The coach is helping players do their jobs.

Name Recognition

Some athletes can capitalize on their name recognition. Basing an income on name recognition can be fragile depending on your behavior and other events. A divorce, DUI, or lawsuit could drag your name through the mud and decrease the value. Basing income on name recognition can be a case of "live by the sword, die by the sword."

FROM ATHLETICS TO BUSINESS

10. Finding the Right Job

Your target job will depend on your education, skills, and passion. If you like what you are going to do you will be motivated to succeed.

Depending on your level of fame, you might find an advantage looking for work in the town where you played sports.

Consider what you have to offer an employer before they tell you what their offer is. Determine your income requirements and desired lifestyle to decide what offer will work best for you.

Sometimes employment can be a springboard for your own business. You can work for a while in the industry to learn the ropes before going out on your own.

People are frequently paid exceedingly diverse salaries for doing about the same jobs. The pay gap between industries, occupations, companies and employees in the same company can be surprising. The amount you will get paid will depend on your education, skills, experience, name recognition value and your negotiating skills.

Be Prepared to Job Search
A job search is much like a full-time job. There are skills required to be successful and land the best opportunity.

The better you develop job hunting skills the sooner you will be working and often the more you will be paid.

Instead of applying randomly at companies and taking the first job offer you receive; develop a line of attack for your search. In other words, work smarter not harder.

Get Organized

Start by making a list of target companies in your field and your networking connections. Keep track of who you contact and when. You can use a computer contacts program, spreadsheet, word documents, or a notebook and pen. Use the method that works best for you.

You will want to keep track of companies, industries, specific job titles, company websites, e-mail addresses, phone numbers, addresses, and contact names. Make contact with people in the companies that interest you. Many people will be happy to speak with you and if your name does carry some weight, they will often even do more for you.

Keep notes of every contact and communication with each person. Many of these people might also be of service at a later time in your career.

What You Need

Small notebooks: Buy several small notebooks so that you can write down everything. Information is everywhere from something on the radio to a conversation at dinner. Be prepared to record this.

Computer and Internet: Make sure you have access to a computer for research, creating your resume, typing cover letters, email communication, and staying organized.

Telephone number and voicemail: A cell phone will work; just make sure your voicemail has a professional greeting. Do not answer the phone while you are busy or in a crowded or loud place. Returning a call when you are prepared rather than being caught off guard can make a big difference in your conversations.

Professional e-mail address: A simple yet professional email address will suffice. Because email accounts are free, set one up specifically for your job search.

High-quality laser printer: You will need to print a resume and cover letter occasionally and should have high-quality text. Laser printers with a minimum of 600 dpi are preferred instead of inkjet and bubble jet printers.

Recording device: Just like watching game tapes, a voice recorder or video camera will allow you to record meetings and listen to yourself so that you can

make improvements. You can also make verbal notes to yourself.

Business cards: Create professional business

cards for your job search that contain all of your contact information. Hand out your cards to everyone of interest that you encounter. Handing out cards may seem uncomfortable at first, but this does pay off.

A reference collection: Reference books

such as a dictionary and thesaurus can help you broaden your vocabulary and improve your writing and conversational skills. Also consider any specialized reference books for your target industry.

Your sanctuary: Create or find a place where

you can work on your job search in peace.

11. Finding the Right Business Venture

Striking out on your own in business will require support from legal counsel and accountants at the very least. They are great to have in your corner from the beginning when you determine your business structure. Your business structure can be a sole proprietorship that comes with great liability, a partnership, or a corporation that offers protection and tax advantages.

Partnerships can be a minefield of problems and should be approached with great care. This is true no matter what relationship you might have with your partner or partners going in. Many a partnership has ended in disaster among the best of friends and spouses.

Many franchises are a cross between business ownership and being an employee. Franchises often come with many restrictions that keep you from ever really being your own boss.

Facing Losses in Businesses

In sports you win some, you lose some, you can tie, and some get rained out. Business is no different.

FROM ATHLETICS TO BUSINESS

When you lose a game in sports are you still analyzing the loss a year later? Probably not. By that time the team members and opponents have changed and a year ago is a lifetime ago in sports. After a loss do you become paralyzed and unable to focus on or play in the next game? If so you will not last long.

The same skills you have acquired that get you through a loss in sports must be utilized to face any defeat in business. Stopping too long to   agonize in business will lead to future losses just as in sports. Regroup after a loss of any kind in business and get rolling again.

More Choices

In addition to selecting the business structure, there are many other choices. For example, buying an existing business can have great advantages over starting a new business when you buy the right business.

An existing business typically already has a positive cash flow or income that a new business can often take years to produce.

Depending on the type of business you go into, you will need to become familiar with contracts, hiring and employee law and procedures, advertising and marketing, property leases, and information relative to the specific type of business.

FROM ATHLETICS TO BUSINESS

You will need to assess the skills required for the type of business you seek and the role you expect to play. Getting to know the business is smart. Even the best managers can leave and you might need to step in while you search for a replacement.

A business that requires employees might bring family and friends out of the woodwork. Think long and hard before involving them in your business. If you do include them, make sure they understand at the time you hire them that if and when you fire them the decision will be strictly business. (And good luck with that!)

12. Great Resources

The Wharton School of Business and the NFL partnered to build a program with the purpose of preparing athletes for retirement. The program works to develop the athlete's marketable job skills transferred from sports and teaches new skills. The program works to build confidence in the transition that prevents the common depression many retired athletes develop.

More than 220 athletes have gone through the program. They learn to transfer the skills they learned in sports and apply them to business and the workplace.

The Professional Athlete Franchise Initiative is a second that helps retired professional athletes in a second career. The organization touts, "a platform for professional athletes to explore the world of opportunities available within the franchise industry, providing education and information about the rules of engagement and mutual responsibilities that are inherent in the franchise business model."

Started by former NFL Quarterback Michael Stone, he has taken his passion for educating retired professional athletes and helping them explore the business world.

While these two organizations specifically assist professional athletes in the transition from sports, many athletes return to school before or at the time of retirement. They utilize the resources for any students available at most colleges.

13. Avoiding Scams

Anyone with money can be a victim of scams and those with large amounts of money or high incomes that are publicized, such as athletes, become high valued targets.

Losing your money will not be the only damage you will suffer. Many athletes who have been scammed often feel shame, guilt, and anger. Most scams will crash sooner or later. Often there is little recourse for recouping any money and sometimes the crook or crooks get away.

Con artists prey first on the young and uneducated. They often take their time to work their scam and eventually promise the world. These con artists come in all shapes and sizes, races, gender, and in most professions. There have been plenty of crooked agents, lawyers, investments bankers, brokers, and accountants.

So the initial line of defense when athletes sign their first contract is to place their money in a safe place and do nothing with it while they become financially educated.

Con artists look to establish friends or associates of the athlete or seek other common ground. They take their time to work their way in. Con artists are often working more than one mark at a time, so just because a friend or associate is working with someone does not make them safe. Con artists are often some of the nicest people

FROM ATHLETICS TO BUSINESS

making them difficult to recognize. Check out the background of anyone you choose to do business with.

Another line of defense is to develop multiple advisors. In order for a scam to work, the con artist must gain control of the money or assets. Before signing anything, the athlete must have several different trusted advisors review the documents. Many athletes have lost their fortunes by signing a power of attorney allowing someone else to make their financial decisions.

Many con artists give to get. They give you cash, gifts, and pick up the bar tab. This can develop a false sense of trust.

Become financially educated and if you do not understand something about a transaction or deal, say no and walk away.

14. Who Succeeded and How

While the stories of turmoil, tragedy, and demise of pro athletes grab the headlines, there are many successful athlete retirement stories.

Tiki Barber

Tiki Barber has had a second career as a sports commentator, as quite a few retired athletes have done.

George Foreman

Who hasn't seen George Foreman hawking the George Foreman Lean Mean Fat-Reducing Grilling Machine? His life after sports has been so successful an entire generation knows him only as a successful pitchman.

Salton paid George $127.5 million to use his name and sales skills. This was one of the biggest athlete endorsement deals in history. In addition he got 40% of the profits that has made him as much as $4.5 million a month. Foreman has made more than $200 million outside the ring, far more than he made fighting.

Jack McDowell

Jack McDowell was a Major League Baseball pitcher for 12 years. He won the American League CY Young award and

The Sporting News Pitcher of the Year award. By 1995 his pitching skills had diminished and he was booed for his performance, resulting in his infamous giving the finger to the crowd. The incident had little effect on his second career. He had been playing the guitar for the rock group Stick figure since 1992 and is still producing music.

Kerri Strug

Kerri Strug retired from gymnastics after being one of the 1996 Olympics "Magnificent Seven," the team that won the gold medal for the United States for the first time in history.

After retiring, Strug became a schoolteacher and also worked in various positions for the US government, such as staff assistant at the Office of Presidential Student Correspondence and presidential appointee to the Justice Department's Office of Juvenile Justice and Delinquency Prevention.

Heath Shuler

Once a quarterback for the Washington Redskins with a 7-year contract worth over $19 million, Heath Shuler failed to live up to expectations and he was out of the NFL after just four years.

After his sports career, Shuler went into real estate and found success. He won a congressional bid in 2007, where he serves today.

FROM ATHLETICS TO BUSINESS

Oscar De La Hoya

While Oscar De La Hoya generated well over half a billion
dollars for pay-per-view fights in his career, making him
the top pay-per-view earner in ring history, in retirement
he released a Grammy-nominated music album "Oscar,"
and his management company, Golden Boy Promotions,
has more than 40 fighters and other businesses that bring
in more than $100 million annually.

John Elway

Since his retirement, John Elway has owned several
businesses and writes an NFL blog. He also founded The
Elway Foundation, a non-profit organization for the
prevention of child abuse.

He owns two restaurants and sold his five car dealerships
for $82.5 million, yet still participates in the car
dealership business.

LeBron James

Drafted directly out of high school, LeBron James earned
$19 million in his first 4 years in the NBA. Before James
even signed a pro sports contract, Nike signed him to a
seven year, $90 million deal. He also owns a marketing

agency that has deals with Nike, Sprite, Glacéau, Bubblicious, and Upper Deck. In 2010, James made $30 million just in endorsements.

Dave Bing

Dave Bing was a seven-time NBA all-star and stands as one of the NBA's 50 greatest players.

In 1980, Bing launched Big Steel in Detroit. By1991 his steel mill was grossing $61 million in annual sales, making his company the 10th largest African American-owned industrial company in the country.

He then started Superb Manufacturing, which is a $28 million-per-year company. He serves as chairman of Bing Group, an automotive supplier, with sales of over $200 million.

15. Conclusion

Athletes are well equipped to succeed financially after their careers have ended. The twelve universal attributes need only be utilized outside the game:

- Accountability
- Attitude
- Character
- Commitment
- Competitive Perseverance
- Confidence Focus
- Leadership
- Passion
- Perseverance
- Pride
- Professionalism
- Team Work

Sooner or later, we all have to step away from our sport, but not necessarily the game. When we apply what we have learned in sports to our lives and post careers, we can often enjoy the thrills of competition using the principles of sports to succeed in other areas.

Awareness: identifying the unique challenges of the professional athlete is half the battle. Taking actions to prevent failure and ensure success, such as outlined in this book, will greatly increase the chances of winning off the field.

Bibliography

ONLINE SERVICES and the WEB:

Delevingne, Lawrence. "10 Ways Sports Stars Go From Riches to Rags." 18 September 2009 < http://www.businessinsider.com/10-ways-sports-stars-destroy-their-finances-2009-9#using-the-wrong-advisors-7#ixzz1LmO1DQXt>

Montero, David. "Foreclosure for ex-Bronco." 3 April 2008 <http://www.rockymountainnews.com/news/2008/apr/03/foreclosure-crisis-catches-ex-bronco-vance-johnson/>

Fusfeld, Adam. "11 Famous Athletes Who Blew Millions Failing At Business." 8 September 2010. <http://www.businessinsider.com/11-famous-athletes-who-blew-millions-failing-at-business-2010-9#lenny-dykstra-refuses-to-admit-that-he-cant-fund-his-magazine-and-brokerage-company-despite-earning-35m-on-the-field-1>

FROM ATHLETICS TO BUSINESS

(source: www.money-zine.com/Financial-Planning/Debt-Consolidation/Consumer-Debt-Statistics)

Beltran, Jess Matthew. "L.A. Lakers: Bill Fith's Two Miracles." 11, May 2011. Bleacher Report http://bleacherreport.com/articles/697409-los-angeles-lakers-witnessing-two-miracles)

Adams, Jay Scott. "Overcoming Obstacles." 11 May 2007. http://theworldlink.com/sports/article_c2ef8b1e-fb2a-5e2b-8d57-f454608f0d44.html)

Athletes for Charity http://www.athletesforcharity.com/foundation.php

Jones, Dr. Stephen. "Athletes Drop Out Rate a Crisis in the Making." http://EzineArticles.com/?expert=Stephen_Jones_Sr

Robertson, Oscar. "The N.B.A.'s Dropouts." 28, June 2007. http://www.nytimes.com/2007/06/28/opinion/28robertson.html

FROM ATHLETICS TO BUSINESS

Smith, Michael David. "Record 56 Players Leave College Early for NFL Draft." 19, January 2011. http://profootballtalk.nbcsports.com/2011/01/19/record-56-players-leave-college-early-for-nfl-draft/

Giles, Steve. "Injuries still cutting baseball careers short." 25, January 2011. http://baltimoresportsreport.com/injuries-still-cutting-baseball-careers-short-11868.html

Ninomiya, Kent. "How Long Is the Average Career of an NFL Player?" 26, April 2011. http://www.livestrong.com/article/15527-long-average-career-nfl-player/#ixzz1Pv2ThkEU

Collegiate Basketball News Co. "Where the NBA Players Come From." 2011. http://rpiratings.com/NBA.html

"Average Major League Baseball Career 5.6 Years, Says New Study." 11, July 2007. (source: Science Daily) http://www.sciencedaily.com/releases/2007/07/070709131254.htm

FROM ATHLETICS TO BUSINESS

"Preparing for Life After Sports" 13, June 2011. http://www.retiredproathleteassistance.com/2011/06/preparing-for-life-after-pro-sports/

Index

Contact Information

Author: Darius Allen
Address: P.O. Box 29331 Dallas, TX 75229
Visit our website:
www.fromathleticstobusiness.com
Email: info@dariusallen.com
Phone: 817.284.8165
Fax: 817.595.6550
Twitter:

www.twitter.com/atobthebook
Facebook:
www.facebook.com/fromathletestobusiness

FROM ATHLETICS TO BUSINESS